AF228915

Household Robots

A&D Xtreme
An imprint of Abdo Publishing | abdobooks.com

abdobooks.com

Printed in the United States of America, North Mankato, MN.
112018
012019

Editor: John Hamilton
Copy Editor: Bridget O'Brien
Graphic Design: Sue Hamilton
Cover Design: Candice Keimig and Pakou Moua
Cover Photo: Moley Robotics
Interior Photos & Illustrations:
Aeolus Robotics-pgs 6 & 7;
AP-pgs 19 & 20-21; Beetl Robotics-pgs 26 & 27;
ECOVACS ROBOTICS-pgs 14 & 15; iRobot-pgs 10-11, 22 & 23;
iStock-pgs 4-5, 8-9, 22 (top inset), 30-31 & 30 (left inset);
Maytronics-pgs 28 & 29; Moley Robotics-pgs 16 & 17;
Robomow-pgs 24 & 25; Shutterstock-pgs 1, 2-3, 10 (inset) & 30 (right inset);
Suitable Technologies/Willow Garage-pgs 18 & 32;
Warner Bros. Animation-pg 6 (top inset);
Yujin Robot-pgs 8 (bottom inset) & 9 (bottom inset).

Library of Congress Control Number: 2018950011
Publisher's Cataloging-in-Publication Data

Names: Hamilton, S.L., author.
Title: Household robots / by S.L. Hamilton.
Description: Minneapolis, Minnesota : Abdo Publishing, 2019 |
    Series: Xtreme robots | Includes online resources and index.
Identifiers: ISBN 9781532118241 (lib. bdg.) | ISBN 9781532171420 (ebook)
Subjects: LCSH: Personal robots--Juvenile literature. | Robots--Juvenile
    literature. | Intelligent personal assistants (Computer software)--
    Juvenile literature. | Robotics--Juvenile literature.
Classification: DDC 629.892--dc23

Contents

Household Robots

Household chores take time and effort. Many people would rather do something else. Engineers and programmers have created robots to help. There are robots designed to clean floors, walls, and windows. Robot chefs can cook everything from pancakes to soup. Mowing the lawn and cleaning the pool are now being done by robots. Helper robots are a welcome addition to today's households.

XTREME QUOTE – "If robots are to clean our homes, they'll have to do it better than a person."
–James Dyson, Inventor
Home Humanoid

Home Cleaning Robots

Rosie the Robot

Rosie the Robot first appeared in Hanna-Barbera's space-age cartoon, *The Jetsons,* in 1962. People loved the robot maid. Everyone believed robots would one day help with household chores. Aeolus Robotics has created a robot that is on its way to becoming today's robot housekeeper.

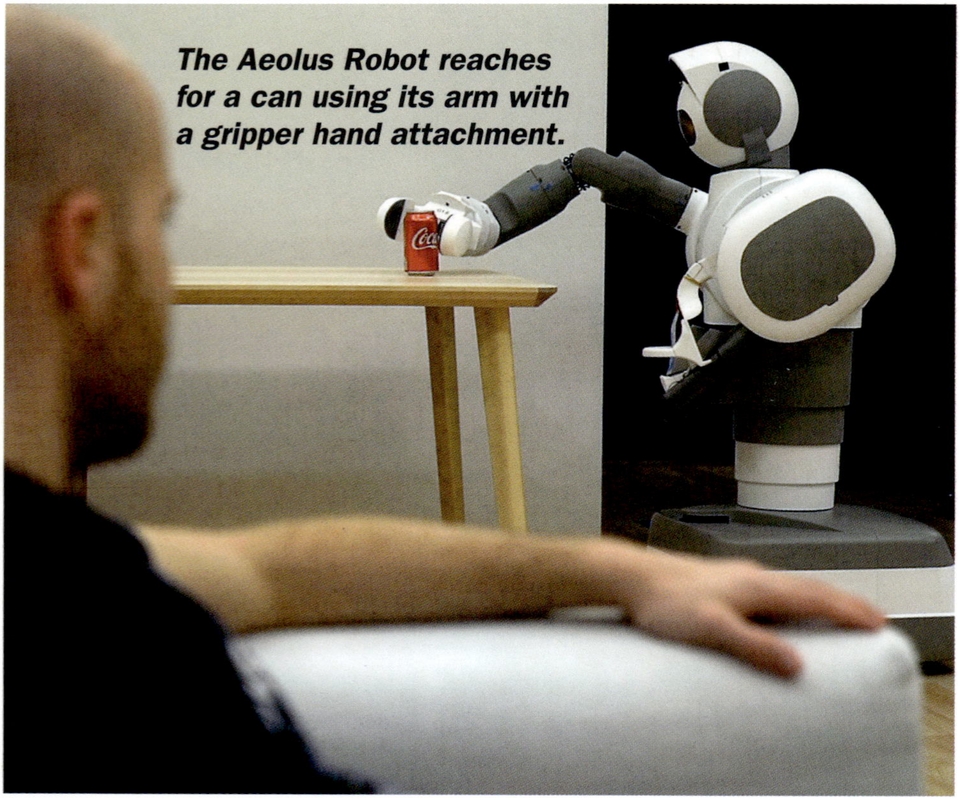

The Aeolus Robot reaches for a can using its arm with a gripper hand attachment.

The Aeolus Robot is programmed to do many different types of work. It has artificial intelligence (AI), or "machine learning," ability. It learns faces and voices of family members, and can respond to voice or text commands. It can recognize and deliver specific food or drinks. It has a long arm for picking up trash from a table or the floor. It can put items away. It can use a vacuum or dry mop to clean floors. It learns the layout of a home and can remember where something was last seen to help people find things. Aeolus Robot may be the "Rosie" people want.

The Aeolus Robot can be told to clean the floor at night. The floor is clean in the morning!

Electrolux of Sweden introduced the
first robot vacuum in 1996. It was called
Trilobite. The American company iRobot
began sales of the Roomba in 2002.
These early vacuums had some problems.
They often left dirty areas, especially
close to walls. Some even fell down stairs
or bumped into objects on the floor.
Modern robot vacuums have advanced
programming, sensors, and brushes to
help make homes much cleaner.

Modern robot vacuums, such as the iCLEBO (Intelligent Cleaning Robot) built by Yujin Robot of South Korea, can clean floors and carpets.

The iCLEBO Omega vacuum can climb over small obstacles, avoid falls, follow a variety of driving patterns, and even go into turbo mode to pick up bigger messes. Robot vacuums are marvels of programming and engineering, designed to make life easier.

Most people do not like mopping floors. Hauling heavy buckets of water and wringing out dirty mops is not fun. Engineers have developed robotic mops that clean floors automatically. The Braava jet by iRobot is designed to clean kitchen and bathroom floors. Braava weighs just 2.7 pounds (1.2 kg). Fill its container with water, attach a cleaning pad, and hit the "clean" button. Braava jet will dry sweep or wet mop, freeing up people to do other things.

Braava jet maps the area it is to clean. Once done, it returns to its starting point. It has "cliff detect," so it knows to stop before falling down stairs.

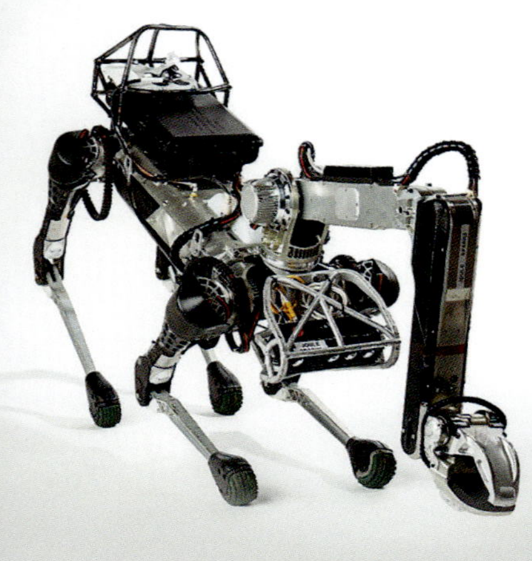

Boston Dynamics knows you can teach a robot dog new tricks. The company's SpotMini is a walking "dog" with a long, jointed arm that looks like a head. The quiet-running electric household robot can pick up and carry objects weighing up to 31 pounds (14 kg). It can operate for 90 minutes before needing to recharge. Its cameras and sensors help it move safely around a house. SpotMini can even pick itself up if it falls. It can also pick up and throw away trash or load a dishwasher. Good dog!

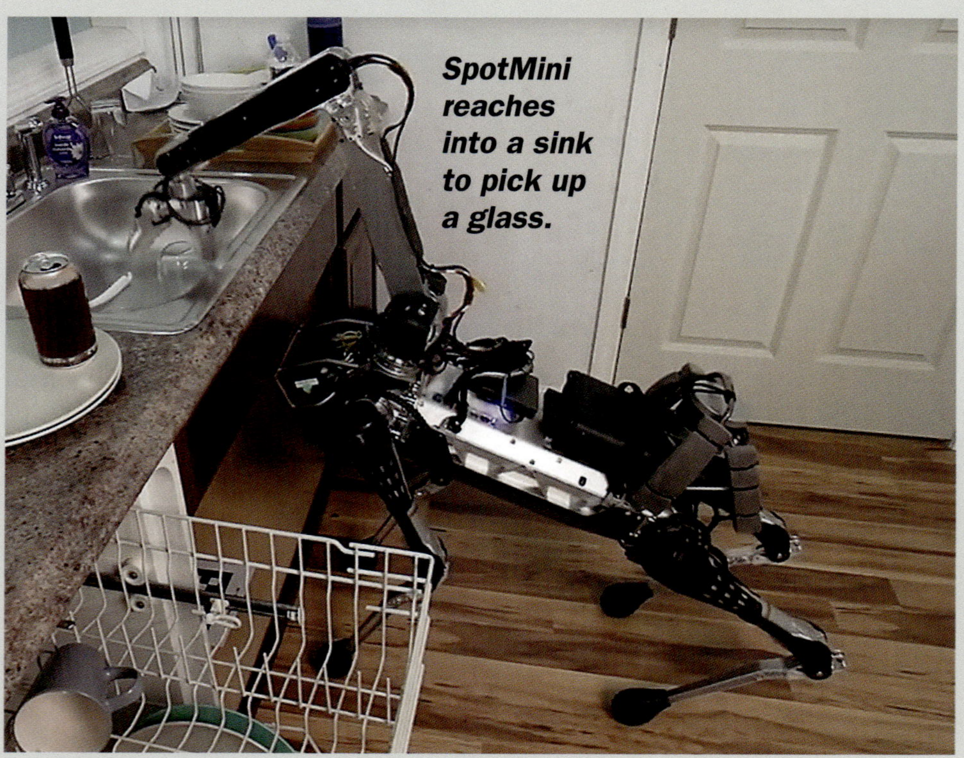

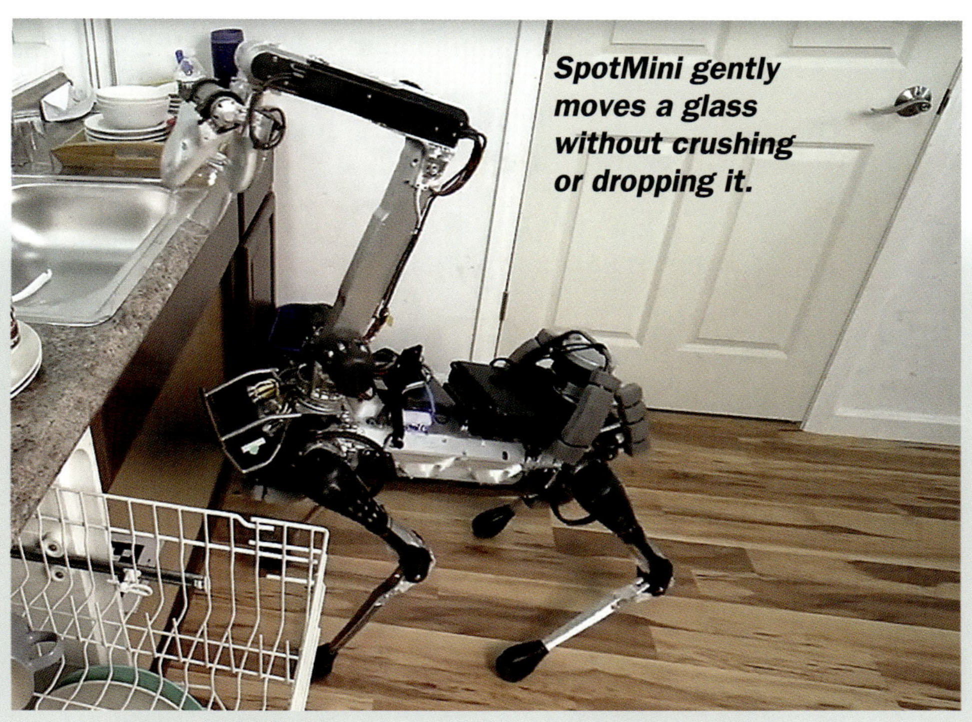

SpotMini gently
moves a glass
without crushing
or dropping it.

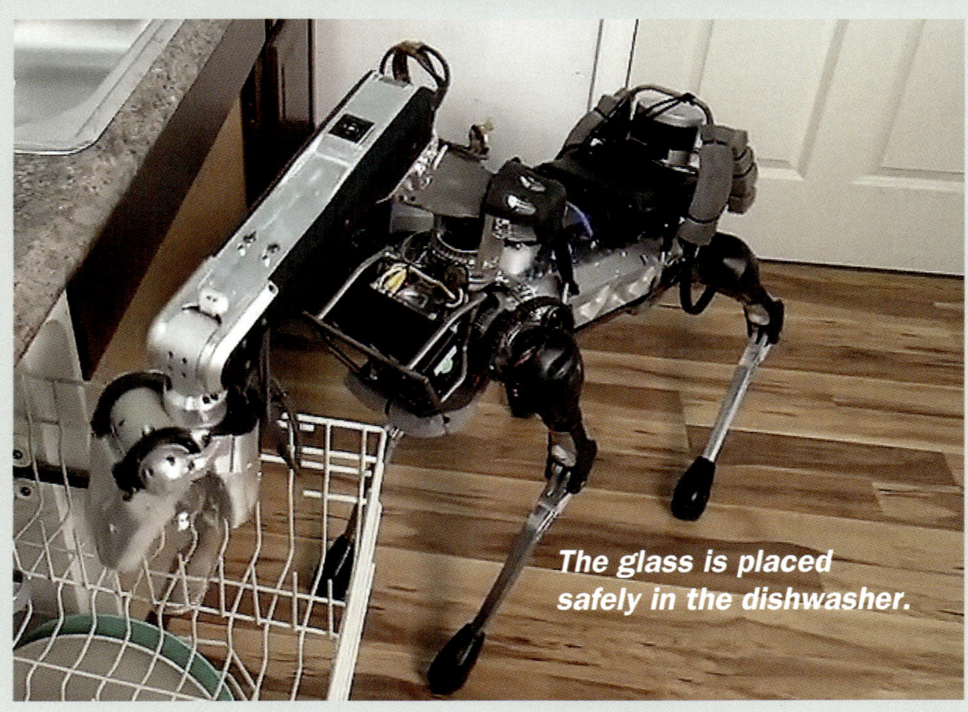

The glass is placed
safely in the dishwasher.

WINBOT X is the first battery-powered, window-cleaning robot. For humans who can't reach tall windows or simply don't like this task, this robot makes life easier. It uses sensors to plot a path across the surface, cleaning as it goes. The WINBOT X is designed to cling to glass with strong suctions. It has a Safety Tether System to keep it from falling. If the tether's suction loosens, an alarm goes off. If the robot's suction loosens, the tether draws back in to prevent WINBOT X from crashing to the ground.

WINBOT X is 7 inches wide by 7 inches long (18 x 18 cm) and cleans glass windows, doors, walls, and tables.

WINBOT X automatically chooses the best path and cleans the entire surface.

Spray WINBOT X with its special glass cleaner. As the robot moves, it squeegees, and wipes, so windows are streak-free. WINBOT X works for 50 minutes on a single charge.

Home Cooking Robots

Everyone loves when someone cooks for them. Moley Robotics has developed the world's first robotic kitchen. Its robot chef works at all hours and doesn't get tired. MK1 is an entire professional kitchen. The kitchen includes all appliances and tools, plus a robot master chef. Although still in development, today it can create and serve a tasty soup. Future plans would allow people to choose from a library of recipes. People can let their MK1 make their meal.

Nimble robot hands, created by Shadow Robot Company, are used in the Moley Kitchen to prepare a meal.

The robot hands can use most kitchen utensils, including spoons, whisks, and knives.

The robot chef serves up a creamy soup. Future versions will allow people to choose what they want the robot to make from a list of recipes.

PR2 (Personal Robot 2) was created by the Willow Garage company in 2010. This helper robot can roll from room to room, as well as grasp and use objects. It can do many household tasks. PR2 is an "open platform" robot. Owners create programs for it. One of its useful abilities is its pancake-cooking talent. PR2 may be programmed to cook other recipes and then clean up. It would be a welcome robot helper.

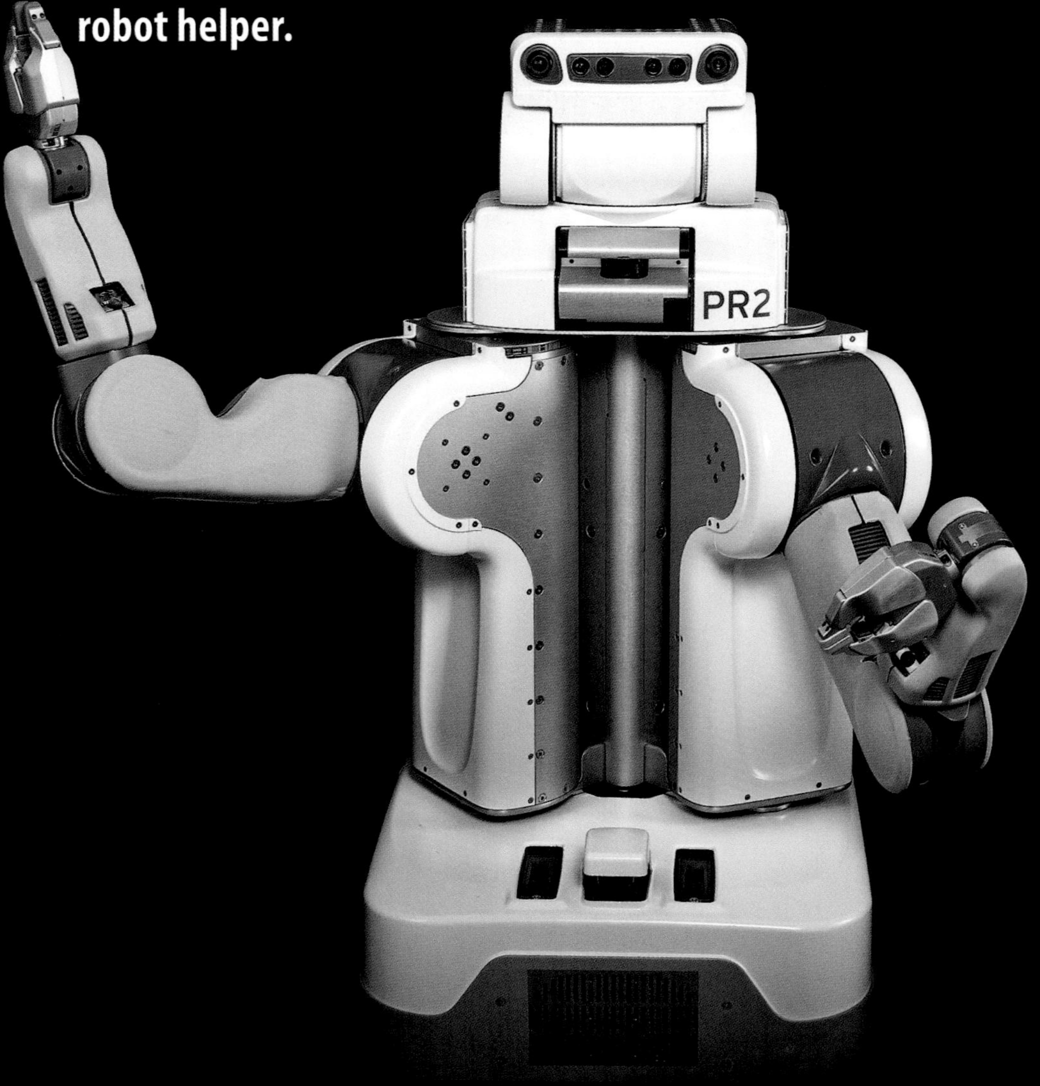

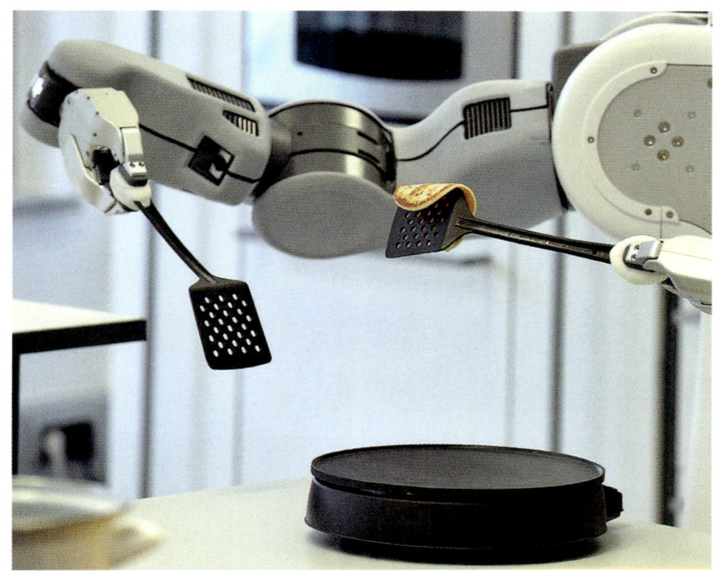

PR2 can hold and grasp utensils such as spatulas and spoons. It has a delicate-enough touch to hold ceramic plates and cups without breaking them.

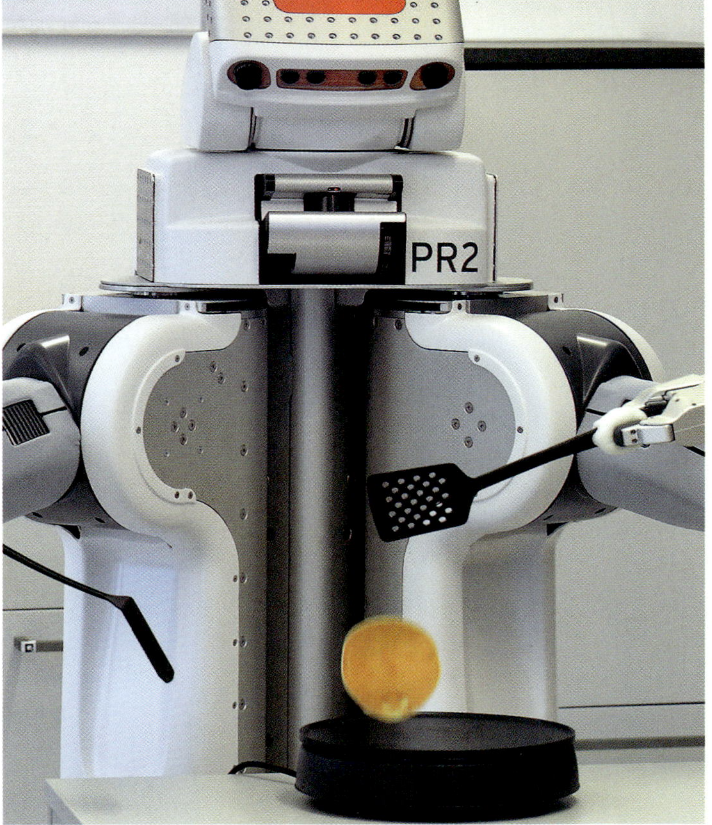

The PR2 helper robot demonstrates its nimble wrists and hands by flipping pancakes. Since it is an open platform robot, it may be programmed to do a wide range of household tasks, including cooking and cleaning.

Outdoor Cleanup & Yard Robots

Some robots are made to help with outdoor chores. They save people time by performing tasks we don't like to do. For example, GrillBot is a grill-cleaning robot that attacks burnt-on food and grease. A push of its start button sends it moving autonomously across the grill. Its three wire brushes spin across the grates. An alert sounds when it's done. To clean the robot's brushes, the owner pops them off and runs them through a dishwasher. GrillBot makes a dirty chore easy.

Cleaning a gutter by hand.

A house's gutters often fill with dead leaves and decaying muck. Cleaning the gutters is a dangerous and disgusting job. A person must carry up a bucket, reach into a gutter, and flick goo into the pail. The person must then climb down, move the ladder, and repeat. Yuck. The Looj gutter cleaner by iRobot is designed to roll along the gutter using an auger-and-brush shape to spin the trough clean.

The iRobot Looj has a clip, so a person doesn't have to hold it when climbing a ladder to place it in the gutter.

The owner goes up the ladder with the Looj and places it in the gutter. After the "clean" button is pressed on the remote control, the Looj moves down the trough and muck flies out! If the robot hits an obstacle, it backs up and tries again.

Robomow is a robot that mows a lawn on a set schedule. Program Robomow to go when you want it to, and then forget it. It starts up, mows the lawn, and then returns to its charging station. Humans can play in the yard instead of mowing it.

Robomow
RS 630
Robomow

There are 35 million households with dogs and backyards in the United States. People love their dogs, but no one likes cleaning up after them. Beetl is a poop-scooping robot. It works autonomously, searching a yard for poop. Once sensors locate a turd, Beetl moves out. It has obstacle avoidance, so it goes around toys, trees, or other objects in a yard. It stops over the poo, drops its clamshell jaws, and scoops up the doggie mess. It then takes and drops the poo into an in-ground composter for disposal.

Beetl's sensors locate poo.

Beetl moves across the yard to the poo.

Beetl positions itself over the poo.

Beetl's clamshell jaws pick up the poo.

Cleaning a pool can be hard, backbreaking work. It takes time, equipment, and patience to do a good job. Today's best robot pool cleaners are designed to put an end to this difficult chore. Maytronics' Dolphin Nautilus is a robot cleaner that scrubs and vacuums the bottom, sides, and waterline of a pool, leaving it super clean. Its navigation system lets it avoid objects in its way and then get back on track, collecting leaves, dirt, and other debris.

The Dolphin Nautilus weighs only 22 pounds (10 kg). This makes it easy to place in the pool. A person starts the robot using a remote control or cell phone program. A filter basket holds the collected debris. Once the robot is finished, the basket lifts out for easy emptying. A quick spray of a hose cleans the basket. Pool cleaning takes about 3 hours, and then the area is ready for swimmers.

Dolphin Nautilus cleans the side of a pool.

Artificial Intelligence (AI)
The ability of a programmed machine or robot to think and learn on its own. Also called "machine intelligence."

Autonomous
Able to work on its own. An autonomous robot does not have a human operator. Its programming allows it to do its job without help.

Charging Station
A place where electricity is available and a robot can recharge its batteries so it can continue operating.

Clamshell
A term that refers to the shape of a clam's shell, as well as how it opens and closes. Clamshell jaws are found on equipment used for picking up materials.

Engineer
A person whose job is to use scientific knowledge to create and maintain mechanical and electronic objects and structures. This includes such things as robots, cameras, and engines.

OBSTACLE AVOIDANCE

The ability to go around, or "avoid," an object that is in the way. Robots are often programmed with obstacle avoidance.

OPEN PLATFORM

When the physical design or "hardware" of a robot is made public so anyone can look at it and create a software program to make the robot perform a specific task. This is also called "open source."

PROGRAMMING

In robots, a language of coded commands and instructions that allow it to perform specific tasks.

SENSORS

In robots, devices that send out signals and get information from a surrounding area. The robot's computers may use the data to decide what the robot should do next, or pass the collected information on to a human operator.

TETHER

A connecting rope or wire. In robots, it may be used to keep an object from moving too far away or as a way to get power to the robot.

To learn more about household robots, visit abdobooklinks.com. These links are routinely monitored and updated to provide the most current information available.

Index